Melissa Naase

The Americans' and Asians' Ideas about Each Other in T.C. Boyle's "East is East"

GRIN Publishing

Bibliographic information published by the German National Library:

The German National Library lists this publication in the National Bibliography; detailed bibliographic data are available on the Internet at http://dnb.dnb.de .

Imprint:

Copyright © 2011 GRIN Verlag, Open Publishing GmbH
Print and binding: Books on Demand GmbH, Norderstedt Germany
ISBN: 978-3-640-97670-6

This book at GRIN:

http://www.grin.com/en/e-book/176392/the-americans-and-asians-ideas-about-each-other-in-t-c-boyle-s-east

GRIN - Your knowledge has value

Since its foundation in 1998, GRIN has specialized in publishing academic texts by students, college teachers and other academics as e-book and printed book. The website www.grin.com is an ideal platform for presenting term papers, final papers, scientific essays, dissertations and specialist books.

Visit us on the internet:

http://www.grin.com/

http://www.facebook.com/grincom

http://www.twitter.com/grin_com

Universität Paderborn

Fachbereich: Anglistik

Sommersemester 2011

The Americans' and Asians' Ideas about Each Other in T.C. Boyle's "East is East"

Melissa Naase

Table of Contents

1 Introduction

This paper is about the stereotypes that Asians and Americans have of each other. Therefore quotations from Boyle's book: "East is East" are listed. Though it was not part of the presentation ,you will also find the quotations on the Asians' ideas about Americans here in order to give a statement on each nation's representative's awareness on those matters.

After that there is a chapter on coping with prejudices, and the terms of assimilation and acculturation are defined.

Last there is an overview of our presentation explaining the different phases, their contents and aims. The transcript of the news-show is given and a short reflection on the presentation and working on this topic can be found.

Before you read on, I would like to explain three terms here which are used simultaneously during this paper. Often it is not possible to distinguish between a *cliché*, a *stereotype* or a *prejudice* because the definitions of those terms are very similar and the choice of the right term depends on everyone's individual experiences with regard to the certain subject.

Nevertheless I want to show that there are certain differences, by giving the definitions here:

- **Cliché**: A phrase or opinion that is overused and shows a lack of original thought.

- **Stereotype**: An image or idea of a particular type of person or thing that has become fixed through being widely held.

- **Prejudice**: Pre-assumption, pre-conceived opinion that is not based on reason or actual experience.

2 Quotes: The Asians' Ideas about Americans

Actually this chapter on the Asian's ideas about Americans was not part of our presentation. But when reading the book I marked all of those in order to compare the stereotypes both nations have of each other.

2.1 Words used for Americans in the Book

- long nose
- hakujin
- butter stinker
- keto (p.267)
- for Saxby: big hairy *boifurendo*

2.2 Hiro's Grandma describing his Father
p.15

..(he always was dirty and hairy, no matter the version)...

2.3 Hiro's View of Americans- Adopted from Films and Books

p.17f

But if Japanes were a pure race, intolerant of misgenation to the point of fanaticism, the Americans, he knew, were a polyglot tribe, mutts and mulattos and worse- or better, depending on your point of view. In America you could be one part Negro, two parts Serbo-Croatian and three parts Eskimo and walk down the street with your head held high. If his own society was closed, the American was wide open- he knew it, he'd seen the films, read the books, listened to the LPs- and anyone could do anything pleased there.

p.46

Pavement. … If he followed it, he reasoned, the road would lead him to civilization, to some tidy little farmhouse where he could risk showing himself and beg for food in exchange for doing odd jobs, maybe sleep in a barn like in those black-and-white movies with the clanking jalopies and the smiling *long-nosed* old ladies in bonnets and dresses that hung to the floor. Or he could find a diner or a McDonald's like the ones in Tokyo-…- he could purchase a meal, fries and a Big Mac, Chicken McNuggets and a shake.

Hiro buying Coke, p.50

Say something, Hiro told himself, say something, and all at once he had an inspiration. Burt Reynolds, Clint Eastwood- what would they say? Americans began any exchange of pleasantries with a string of courses, anyone knew that- and even if he hadn't- known it, even if he were an innocent, he'd seen Eastwood in action. "Mothafucka," he said, bowing to the girl as he shuffled forward to dump his

3

booty on the counter. And to the bewildered boy, in the most amenable tone he could summon, he observed: "Cocksucka, huh?"

p.52

He knew them. Americans. They killed each other over dinner, shot one another for sport, mugged old ladies in the street. Help like that he didn't need.

p.196f

He knew them. They'd tried to run him down before he'd even set foot on their soil, they'd chase him out of Hog Hammock and Ambly Wooster's house too. They were Americans. Killers. Individualists gone rampant. He hung his head and started for the door.... expecting no mercy but the law of the jungle and of the mutt and half-breed.

2.4 Hiro's Impressions of America

p.136

To be here, inside, with rugs on the floors and paintings on the walls, to be here at the center of all this wonderful immensity, all this living space- this was paradise, this was America.

p.144

But still, the Americans made such a mess of their food—just served it in a heap, with no thought of grace or proportion, as if eating were a shameful thing- and if he weren't starving, he would have turned up his nose at it.

p.226

The fools. They were so stupid it was incredible. Four hours they'd sat there, and never once did they glance up at the window. The was the American nature. They were oafs, drugged and violent and overfed, and they didn't pay attention to detail. That's why the factories had shut down, that's why the automakers had gone belly up, that's why thee professional investigators could sit in an eight-by-ten-foot cell for four hours and never notice that two of the bars had been pried from the window.

p.268

...there was nothing but water, muck, creeper and vine, the damnable unending fetid stinking wilderness of America. But no, it couldn't be. Was it all swamp, the whole hopeless country? Where where the shopping malls, the condos, the tattoo parlors and supermarkets? Where the purple mountains and the open range? Why couldn't the butter-stinker have popped open the trunk at the convenience store, at Burger King or Saks Fifth Avenue? Why this? ...

2.5 The Japanese's Point of View about Negros
p.42

Worse: the stranger was a black man, a Negro, and he knew, as every Japanese does, that Negros were depraved and vicious, hairier, sweatier and even more potent than their **white counterparts**, the *hakujin*. They were violent and physical, they were addicted to drugs and they thought only with their sexual organs.

2.6 Hiro's American Hopes

p.95

... and he was free- or he would be, if only he could get to Beantown or the City of Brotherly Love[1]... every face was different- they were white and black and yellow and everything in between- and they all glowed with the rapture of brotherly love.

p.99

What was he going to do- grow a long black beard and eat dirt all his life, live like a caveman or a hippie or something? No, he had to go to Beantown, the Big Apple, to the City of Brotherly Love; he had to blend in with the masses, find himself a job, an apartment with western furniture and Japanese appliances, with toaster ovens and end tables and deep thick woolly carpets that climbed up the walls like surging tide. Then he'd be sage, then he could play miniature golf and eat cheeseburgers or stroll down the street with an armload of groceries and no one would blink twice.

2.7 Ruth talking about the Asians Ideas of Americans
p.261

"The U.S. Marines were about to land and the civilians had been abandoned. The rumor was that to become a Marine you had to murder your own parents. Can you imagine that?- that's what they thought of us. The Japanese- *civilians*, women and children- leaped from a cliff into the sea rather than fal into the hands of such monsters.

---

[1] It is merely a translation of the Greek phrase "brotherly love" from philos "love" and adelphos "brother"→ Philadelphia.

3 Quotes: The Americans' Ideas of Asians

3.1 Words used for Asians in the Book

- **Nip:** (U.S. and UK) A derogatory term for someone of Japanese descent (shortened version of *Nipponese*, from the Japanese name for Japan, *Nippon*)
- **Gook:** Like the German "Schlitzauge"

3.2 Outward Appearance

Ruth and Saxby look at Hiro: p.10

The light was in her lap, the breeze gave her a scent of the shore. "Yes," she said finally, "Chinese."

Ruth writes on her novel about a Japanese woman who kills herself and remembers Hiro. p.27

Chinese. She'd thought he was Chinese. But then she'd never traveled any farther east than sushi bars of Little Japan or the chop suey houses of Chinatown, and to this point in her life she'd never had any need to differentiate one nationality from another. If the sign outside said Vietnamese, then they were Vietnamese; if it said Thai, then they were Thai.

Ruth catches Hiro on her porch. p.66

He didn't even look Japanese, with his tan irises and dull reddish hair, or did he? There were the epicanthic folds she remembered from anthropology, the round face and stutter nose, the bow legs and the too-deep tan of his scraped and bitten limbs. Blink once and he was Toshiro Mifune; blink again, and he was something else.

Before the interrogation of Hiro p.234

Six weeks to nail one sorry slump-shouldered fat-assed Nip who looked like he was about twelve years old.

Hiro is helped by some campers when he comes from the Okefenokee p.281

"You are a Filipino?"

3.3 Food

Ruth writes in her novel about a Japanese woman who kills herself and remembers Hiro.p.27

She knew Asians only as people who served dishes with rice.

Ruth wants to surprise Hiro by bringing him what she considers the favorite Japanese food. p.190

He was expecting a treat- a wedge of cake or a Mars Bar maybe; she knew he loved Mars Bars- but she dug yet another can of fried dace and a cellophane package of withered roots from the depths of the bag. His face fell. How she'd ever got the idea that this- this *stuff*-would appeal to him was a mystery. Dried fishheads, bark shavings in plastic envelopes, flat black mushrooms like patches of sloughed skin, can after can of bamboo shoots- what did she think he was, some barefoot hick from

Tohoku or something?[…] He would have preferred practically anything- Chef Boyardee, Hamburger Helper, Dinty Moore- but it was too awkward to ask. Beggars couldn't be choosy.

The police questioning Ruth p.206

"About the food. We found- what do you call it-*Oriental* food-stuffs on the premises, seaweed and dried roots and suchnot. […]"

3.4 Cultural Prejudice

What Detlef thinks of Japanese' illegal country entrance p. 56

They never entered the country illegally. Didn't want to. They figured they had it all and more over there, so why bother? Plenty of them came in to run factories and open banks and whatnot, but all that was done at the highest levels.

What Turco Abercorn's assistant thinks about Japanese people p.61-62

"What you got to realize about the Nips is they're the squarest people in the world, I mean the hokiest, bar none. Shit, even the paddy Burmese are downtown compared to the Japs. They're all part of this like big team, this like Eagle Scout thing where everybody fits in and works real hard and makes this perfect and totally unique society. Because they are superior to everybody else, they're purer- that's what they think. Nobody but Japanese in Japan. You fuck up, you let the whole race down."[…] "Even the far- out types, the rebels, the punks with the orange hair and the leather jackets- and there are precious few of them, believe me- even they can't break the mold. You know they get down, you know how they really thumb their nose at society and show what bad characters they are?"[…] "They all go down to Yoyogi Park in Tokyo on Saturday afternoon from one to three and turn up their boom boxes and dance. That's it. They dance. All of them. Squarest people in the world."

"So, uh, what do you think we ought to do? […] The Nips- the Japanese, I mean- tend to be pretty fanatical too, don't they? *Hara-kiri, kamikazes,* the human wave and all of that?"

"Yeah, I've been to the movies too. But the fact is, like I told you, they're just plain square. You know how to catch this clown?"

"No."

"You know what I got in there? A boom box. Sanyo. Biggest shitkicker you ever saw, puts out enough amps to kill every woodpecker out there stone dead in two minutes flat. I've got a couple disco tapes, Michael Jackson, Donna Summer, that kind of shit, you follow me? I'm going to track the fucker, no different than if this was 1966 in the Ia Drang Valley, cross a trail, any trail. Then I'm going to set this thing on a stump and crank it up."

The old lady who mistakes Hiro for Seiji

p.133

" You are so clever, you Japanese, what with your automobile factories and your Suzuki method and that exquisite Satsuma ware- busy as a hive of bees, aren't you? You've even got whiskey now, so they tell me, and of course you've got your beers- your Kirin and your Suntory and your Sapporo- and they're every bit as good anything our lackadaisical brewing giants have been able to produce, but *sake, sake* I could never understand, how *do* you drink that odious stuff? And your educational system, why, it's the wonder of the world, engineers and scientists and chemists and what have you, and all because you're not afraid of work, back to the basics and all of that. You know, sometimes I almost wish you *had* won the war- I just think it would shake this spineless society up, [...], but of course you have no crime whatsoever, do you? I've walked the streets of Tokyo myself, at the witching hour and past it, [...], helpless as I am, and nothing, nothing did I find but courtesy, courtesy, courtesy- manners, that's what you people are all about. [...] I think I can appreciate how you must feel, a defeated nation, after all. [...]"

p.135

[...] I mean the Japanese don't even *have* bedrooms- [...]. But then, where *do* your sick and elderly lie up when they're ailing?... I suppose in those excellent hospitals, best in the world, *our* medical profession certainly can't touch them, what with the AMA and all their infighting,our students having to attend medical school in Puerto Rico and Mexico and all those filthy, horrid, Third World places-"

Ruth to Hiro p.135

"You read English?"

Hiro thanks Ruth for her help p.154

"I can never repay my debt to you, not in a hundred lifetimes."

"Forget it," she said, "you would do the same for me- anybody would." She didn't know exactly what she meant by that, but she could feel his embarrassment, some sort of macho Japanese thing, she supposed [.][...]

Roy, a friend of Saxby p.321

"[...] From what I've heard of the Japanese-they're pretty resourceful, aren't they?"[...] "Still and all, I'd wager they haven't got anything like this over there, and resourcefulness can only take you so far, know what I mean?"'

3.5 People of a lower Class

Ruth caught Hiro on her porch.

I want to make you my own.

p.69

[...] an exotic and fascinating creature, yes, but not yet her own, not yet her sword and wedge and bludgeon to lay Thanatopsis House at her feet.

p.119

For a moment the thought arrested her: he *was* a tomcat, a mercenary, and he didn't give a damn for all the risc she'd taken to get him clean change of clothes or the sacrifice of forging her lunch all this time.

Ruth's excuses for hiding Hiro p.204

"He was just- it was like a stray dog or something."

Hunting Hiro p.216

They showed him, abused him, humiliated him, made him walk the gauntlet of them as if they were red Indians in the forest, jeering and spitting and cursing him for a Jap, a Nip, a gook and a Chinaman.

Before the interrogation of Hiro p.224

[...] but they wouldn't listen, didn't care, caught the vaguest glimmer of what he was saying and shouted him down.

Breaking News in a newspaper p.288

"Score I for the Japanese, 0 for the INS; 'Jailbreak on Tupelo Island: Alien Makes It Look Easy' "

Ruth imagines Hiro as somebody who got shipwrecked and needs help. In the evening during a party in Thanatopsis House.p.30

She'd watched an exhausted, half-hysterical survivor flounder to shore and flail through the bushes in a panic. And all they could do was make Chinese jokes.

3.6 The Danger created by Foreigners

Hiro escaped to Tupelo Island because he feared that Americans might murder him. Here is what the authorities think of Hiro. p.28

He was believed to be armed and dangerous.

Detlef Abercorn is responsible for the arrest of Hiro.p.54

From the Chief Engineer of the Japanese ship- a desiccated old fart about a hundred and twelve years old who looked as if he'd been hatched from an egg- he learned that the man at large was armed with a knife and had attacked half the ship's crew before throwing himself over the rail, and so he'd had the regional head upgrade the designation to IAAD, Armed and Dangerous. Still, it was no big deal. A Nip in Georgia? These people [in Georgia] ate weasel, picked their teeth with their feet, grew right up out of the ground like weeds, like kudzu; the poor dumb Nip-Japanese- wouldn't last a day, six hours even.

Before the interrogation of Hiro p.222

For a long moment the three of them stood in the doorway, watching him as they might have watched a tethered animal, as if trying nd how to gauge how dangerous he might be and how far and suddenly he might leap.

Park where one can rent canoes: Rumours about Hiro p.297

"Killed somebody east of here, is what I heard,"[...]

"Three grown men and a baby. Strangled them all,"[...]

4 Awareness of Prejudices

Although prejudices against the other nation can be found on both- the Asians' and the Americans' – sides, the awareness about the prejudices is different.

Hiro knows that Ruth has prejudices against him. He experiences this all the time. He never asked for the Asian food Ruth buys for him all the time and he does not like it. He also is aware of the prejudice that all Asians look the same . He makes use of this to get food and a place to sleep when he meets the old lady who mistakes him for an Asian guy she hardly knows.[2]

He is also aware of the stereotype that Chinese do not speak English. He experiences this during his imprisonment when the policemen talk to each other as if Hiro were not present.

On the other hand Ruth is not aware of the prejudices Hiro has about the Americans. Of course, Hiro is alone in a foreign country and in a different position than Ruth is. He is thankful for Ruth's help though she makes him angry on some occasions. But he never shows her what his ideas about the Americans are. As Ruth is in a more powerful situation Hiro gets to know what she thinks about Asians.

5 Coping with Prejudices- The Assimilation vs. Acculturation Debate

In America there live 11.9 million people in America who identify themselves as Asian-Americans. 85.7 % of them have purely Asian heritage and 14.3% mixed heritage. 71.4% of the Asian-Americans speak English „very well" and only 46% speak an Asian language at home. Another interesting fact is that in 2003 50% of Asian-Americans had a bachelor degree and the rate is climbing.[3]
Those Asian-Americans have different ways of coping with their situations. Whilst many "only" acculturate others cannot live there without assimilating.

Assimilation means that it allows one's original culture to be overridden by the dominant culture.
Acculturation means acquiring the capability to function within the dominant culture while retaining one's original culture.

In the book, Hiro sticks with his culture; he would never assimilate, instead he prefers dying the way a samurai does.

6 Structure and Aims of the Presentation

The topic of the presentation was "The American's ideas about the Asians". To make it more interesting and offer a topic for a discussion we also added the topic "assimilation vs. acculturation",

---

[2] Seji is a famous conductor (Boston Symphony)
[3] vgl. http://goldsea.com/Air/Issues/Identity/identity.html (02.07.2011)

because we wanted to connect the topic of the presentation to something which would provide room for a discussion in class.

This chapter gives an overview of the schedule for our presentation. In the table below you also find the intentions/aims of each phases, their contents and outcome.

Phase *intentions*	Content	Outcome
Introduction *Activating pre-knowledge, warming up,*	Brainstorming, Mind Map on the board	The prejudices we have about the Asians are similar to those Ruth has
Main part *Input, reorganizing the given information from the book*	The news broadcast	Summary on the board: Stereotypes found in the book
Group work- discussion *Establishing your own opinion and discussing it with other students*	Intro Assimilations vs. Acculturation Video: plastic surgery in order to assimilate with the Americans[4] Discussion topic: What are the advantages and disadvantages of retaining their identities as Asians in a white- majority society? What's the price paid by those who choose to assimilate? What's better for the U.S. as a nation?	Discussion in groups and later in class: -Finding a way to stay oneself -how far should one go in order to integrate in to a foreign nation?

Transcript of the News broadcast:

Barnie: Good evening Ladies and Gentlemen. Today we dedicate our broadcasting time to the latest incidents concerning the American-Japanese alliance. It is not enough that the Japanese market threatens the US economy, moreover recent incidents have shown that Japan plans to infiltrate our country from inside.

Their project is called The Nip-Gook-Tomcat-Chinese, alias Hiro Tanaka. This armed and dangerous man came ashore on Tupelo Island. Police have put several efforts into catching Tanaka. For this reason, Detlef Abercorn and Turco Lewis developed a highly effective method called "The Boom box West Strategy". Our reporter Janice Simpson interviewed Mr. Lewis in the afternoon. Janice please tell us how this method works.

Janice:" Well Barnie, this highly efficient idea was developed by Mr. Turco himself. I am glad we have such good technology in our country. It works like this: You place a boom box in the forest and play all those amazing hits these Asian folks like. (Sorry for that but to me they all look the same.) So you let Donna Summer or Michael Jackson be fuddle Japanese senses and voila, you got them. Boy they

---

[4]vgl. http://www.goldsea.com/Video//video/294/Asian-Eyelid-Surgery (02.07.2011)

are crazy about American stuff. To make the bait more attractive, just put a nice T-shirt with *Keep On Truckin'* on it and those guys come like bees for honey.

Barnie:" Has the police already tried this technique on Tanaka?

Janice:" No, not yet. First of all, they have to plan ahead. Those Asians are clever. Their educational system is brilliant. They have these huge automobile factories and super hospitals. Moreover, they seem to function like a bee hive as experts report. For that reason, police has to be careful not to raise suspicion. The boom box has to be placed in the wood as inconspicuous as possible.

Barnie: "Thank you Janice. And now we come to the interview with the unpatriotic woman who gave this Chinese man refuge. Let's directly switch to Tupelo Island where the unpatriotic woman, Ruth Dershowitz, who gave Tanaka refuge is waiting to be interviewed. Hallo Ruth, do you feel bad about giving refuge to the most dangerous man in the world?

Ruth: I am sorry to interrupt but I didn't give refuge to anybody. You just have to take a look on this exotic and fascinating creature of Hiro Tanaka. I just wanted to make him my own, to use him for my new story. He was like a stray dog or something.

Barnie: So you deny that you bought him all the oriental food which was found in your apartment? I mean the withered roots, rice, dried fish heads and stuff like flat black mushrooms.

Ruth: I don't deny anything. I bought him food but did not have any other contact. He just came into my apartment, when I wasn't at home. I am so damn innocent. Consider this, I thought he was Chinese. I mean I have never travelled any farther than Chinatown and to this point never had to differentiate between Asians but this man definitely seemed to be Chinese and looked poor. Like a wild animal that needs to be stroked.

Barnie: So you don't feel ashamed for your deed.

Ruth: Which deed? I am an artist; I need inspiration to create my great novels.

Barnie: Ok this conversation is pointless. This woman does not feel guilty of anything. Now let us go back to the important issues.

Oh good news! We just received the information that Tanaka has been captured in the swamp of the Okefenokee. As we know the Japanese work in teams. They are highly organized like an Eagle Scout troop and this means there will come more of them. More dangerous Aliens like Tanaka. Never before, Asians entered America illegally. But now times have changed and we return back to the Cold War with the new enemy: Japan.

So here are some guidelines how to stay safe:

1) According to anthropology, Japanese have a round face and a stutter nose, bow legs and too-deep tan.

2) They are all into courtesy. So don't let them bewitch you with their manners and their politeness. Keep in mind that they are fanatical; which means meaning: Kamikaze and Hara-kiri.

3) Moreover, these people speak English and can camouflage as US citizen. They are pretty resourceful, so do not try to stop them on your own.

7 Conclusion- Reflections on the Group Presentation

The outcome of the presentation was like what we expected. The main opinion of the seminar was that one must not assimilate but find a way to feel confident in a foreign country. The topic of eyelid-surgery got all the students talking and we had a great discussion. All members of my group enjoyed doing this presentation because it was quite easy for us to encourage the rest of the class to work with us from the start of the presentation to the very end. We all liked the topic we chose because it is a topic concerning everyone and we also found a great internet source which provided us with more material and a video which we used for the discussion. As you can find prejudices, clichés and stereotypes everywhere I appreciate it, that Boyle picked this topic for his novel.

I liked the book, though I found it hard to read in some chapters, especially because it nearly missed direct speech. But it was great to see that nothing in the book was without intention and how Boyle manages to connect so many references in the book. As the book is about stereotypes one should expect Boyle to select a typical identity to represent a nation. But this is not what Boyle did. He picked a samurai to represent the Asian and a Jew to represent the American identity. This shows very clearly that stereotyping does not only exist with the "average American or Asian" but is really omnipresent.

8 Bibliography

- T.C. BOYLE: *East is East*, Bloomsbury Publishing; Auflage: Export Edition (2. Februar 2004)

Internet Sources:

- http://www.goldsea.com/Video//video/294/Asian-Eyelid-Surgery (02.07.2011)

- http://goldsea.com/Air/Issues/Identity/identity.html (02.07.2011)